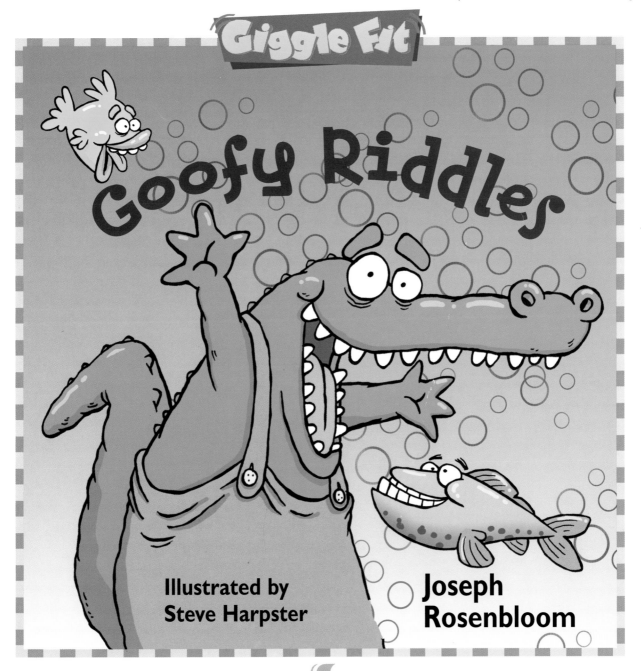

Giggle Fit

Goofy Riddles

**Illustrated by
Steve Harpster**

**Joseph
Rosenbloom**

Sterling Publishing Co., Inc. New York

Library of Congress Cataloging-in-Publication Data

1   3   5   7   9   10   8   6   4   2

Published by Sterling Publishing Company, Inc.
387 Park Avenue South, New York, N.Y. 10016
© 2001 by Joseph Rosenbloom
Distributed in Canada by Sterling Publishing
c/o Canadian Manda Group, One Atlantic Avenue, Suite 105
Toronto, Ontario, Canada M6K 3E7
Distributed in Great Britain and Europe by Chris Lloyd at Orca
Book Services, Stanley House Fleets Lane, Poole BH15 3AJ, England
Distributed in Australia by Capricorn Link (Australia) Pty. Ltd.
P.O. Box 704, Windsor, NSW 2756 Australia
Printed in China
All rights reserved

Sterling ISBN 0-8069-8017-6

How many balls of string would it take to reach the moon?
One, if it were long enough.

What do astronauts eat off?
Flying saucers.

What is an astronaut's favorite meal?
Launch.

How do you put a baby astronaut to sleep?
You rock-et.

What prehistoric animal made noises in its sleep?
The dino-snore.

What would you get if a dinosaur stepped on your foot?
Ankylosaurus.

Where did prehistoric animals go for sun and fun?
To the dino-shore.

How long are a dinosaur's legs?
Long enough to reach the ground.

What newspapers do
dinosaurs read?
The Prehistoric Times.

How do you tell a dinosaur to hurry up?
You say, "Shake a leg-o-saurus!"

Why did the dinosaur cross the road?
Because in those days they didn't have chickens.

What does a shark eat
with peanut butter?
Jellyfish.

Where is the ocean deepest?
On the bottom.

What would you get if you crossed an
octopus and a cow?
An animal that could milk itself.

What would you get if you crossed an octopus and a cat?
**I don't know what you'd call it, but it would have
eight arms and nine lives.**

What would you get if you crossed a shark and a parrot?

An animal that talks your ear off.

What is quicker than a fish?
The one who catches it.

How do babies swim?
They do the crawl.

What do sea monsters have for lunch?
Fish and ships.

What newspaper do cows read?
The Daily Moos.

Why shouldn't you tell a secret to a pig?
Because it is a squealer.

What would you get if you crossed a wolf and a rooster?
An animal that howls when the sun rises.

If a farmer raises corn in dry weather, what does he raise in wet weather?
An umbrella.

If you put three ducks in a carton, what would you get?

A box of quackers.

What did the chickens do in the health club?

Eggs-ercise.

What would you get if you crossed a clock and a chicken?

An alarm cluck.

Which side of a chicken has the most feathers?

The outside.

What insect can be spelled
with just one letter?
Bee.

What do you call a young bee?
A babe-bee.

What would you get if you
crossed an insect and a
rabbit?
Bugs Bunny.

Why do bees hum?
Because they don't know the words.

What kind of gum
do bees chew?
Bumble gum.

What did the bee say to the flower?
"Hello, honey!"

What would you get if you crossed a dog and a waffle?
A woofle.

What do you have to know before teaching tricks to a dog?
More than the dog.

What do you call a dog that graduates from medical school?
Dog-tor.

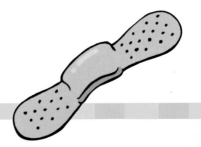

How do dogs travel?
By mutt-a-cycle.

Why do dogs scratch themselves?
Because they are the only ones who know where it itches.

What is the best year
for a kangaroo?
Leap year.

Why did the kangaroo
mother scold her child?
**For eating crackers
in bed.**

Why do mother kangaroos hate rainy days?
Because then the children have to play inside.

What is the difference between a mailbox and a
kangaroo?
**If you don't know, remind me not to give you
any letters to mail.**

What would you get if you crossed a kangaroo and a computer?

An animal that would always be jumping to conclusions.

What would you get if you crossed a kangaroo and a crocodile?

Leaping lizards!

Where does a kangaroo go when it gets sick?

To the hop-ital.

How mad can a kangaroo get?

Hopping mad!

What would you call a lion tamer who puts his right arm down a hungry lion's throat?
Lefty.

Do giraffes have babies?
No, they only have giraffes.

Why is it dangerous to do math in the jungle?
Because if you add 4 and 4, you get 8.

What kind of leopard has red spots?
A leopard with measles.

What would you get if you crossed a laughing hyena with a cat?

A giggle puss.

What would you get if you crossed a woodpecker and a lion?

An animal that knocks before it eats you.

Is it hard to spot a leopard?

No, they come that way.

What do birds say on Halloween?
"Twick or tweet!"

What do little ghosts chew?
Boo-ble gum.

Why did Dracula go to the orthodontist?
To improve his bite.

Where do ghosts mail their Christmas cards?
At the ghost office.

What do you do with a
blue monster?
Cheer him up.

What do ghosts have
with meatballs?
Spook-ghetti.

What do ghosts wear when it rains?
Ghoul-ashes.

What do baby ghosts wear when it rains?
Boo-ties.

What do witches eat at cookouts?
Halloweenies.

Where do witches go
when they get sick?
**To the witch
doctor.**

What do witches eat for breakfast?
Scrambled hex.

How can you tell twin witches apart?
It's not easy to tell which witch is which.

What is the first safety rule for witches?
Don't fly off the handle.

What part of a car causes the most accidents?
The nut behind the wheel.

Do you have to be rich to ride in your own carriage?
Not if you're a baby.

Why did the traffic light turn red?
So would you if you had to change in front of all those people.

Why did the elephant lie in the middle of the road?
To trip the ants.

If you crossed King Kong and a bell, what would you have?
A ding-dong King Kong.

What is brown, has a hump, and lives at the North Pole?
A lost camel.

Why did the otter cross the road?
To get to the otter side.

What would you get if you crossed a chef and a rooster?
Cook-a-doodle-doo.

What food is good for the brain?
Noodle soup.

Why shouldn't you cry over spilled milk?
It gets too salty.

What would you get if you crossed a cocker spaniel, a poodle, and a ghost?
A cocker-poodle-boo!

What is the difference between a stupid person and a pizza?

One is easy to cheat and the other is cheesy to eat.

What do cats put on their hot dogs?

Mouse-tard.

What is the best way to see flying saucers?

Scare the waitress.

What can you find in the Great Wall of China that the Chinese never put there?
Cracks.

What kind of geese are found in Portugal?
Portu-geese.

Where is Timbuktu?
Between Timbuk-one and Timbuk-three.

What flies without
wings, propellers,
or jets?
   Time.

What is a twip?
   **A twip is what a wabbit takes
   when he wides a twain.**

What can you break without touching?
   A promise.

What does the Invisible Man drink at snacktime?

Evaporated milk.

Why did the teacher excuse the little firefly?

Because when you've got to glow, you've got to glow.

How do we know that owls are smarter than chickens?

Have you ever heard of Kentucky Fried Owl?

What did the little skunk
want to be when it grew up?
A big stinker.

What do people make that
you can't see?
Noise.

Why was the little lamb sent to
the principal's office?
Because it was baa-d.

Why are clocks always tired?

You would be too if you had to run all day.

What is gray and blue and very big?

An elephant holding its breath.

Why is an elephant gray, large, and wrinkled?
Because if it were small, white, and round, it would be an aspirin.

Why did the horse sneeze?
Because it had a little colt.

What did one elevator say to the other elevator?
"I think I'm coming down with something."

What is black and white
and red all over?
A sunburned zebra.

What else is black and
white and red all over?
**A skunk with
diaper rash.**

What did the duck say when it fell in love with a parrot?
"Quacker wants a Polly."

What would you get if Minnehaha married Santa Claus?
Minnehaha hoho.

What sound do two porcupines make when they kiss?
"Ouch!"

When do pigs give their girlfriends presents?
On Valen-swine's Day.

Who does the ocean date?
It goes out with the tide.

What kind of children would the Invisible Man and the Invisible Woman have?
I don't know, but they wouldn't be much to look at.

How can you tell that an elephant is visiting your house?

His tricycle is parked outside.

How can you tell that an elephant is in your refrigerator?

The door won't shut.

What room has no walls, no doors, no windows, and no floors?

A mushroom.

How many bricks does it take to finish a house?
Only one — the last one.

In what kind of home do the buffalo roam?
A very dirty one.

What did the mirror say
to the dresser?
"I see your drawers."

What did one garbage
can say to the other?
**Nothing. Garbage
cans can't talk.**

Where does a vampire take a bath?
In the bat-room.

What musical instrument is
found in the bathroom?
A tuba toothpaste.

When a dirty kid has finished taking a bath, what
is still dirty?
The bathtub.

What animal do you look like when you're in the bathtub?
A little bear.

What is the best thing to eat in the bathtub?
Sponge cake.

What is the best way to avoid wrinkles?

Don't sleep in your clothes.

Why do we buy clothes?
Because we can't get them free.

What is the saddest piece of clothing?
Blue jeans.

What always speaks the truth but doesn't say a word?
A mirror.

What did the wig say to the head?
"I've got you covered."

What do frogs wear on their feet in the summer?
Open toad shoes.

What would you get if you sawed a comedian in half?
A half wit.

What would you get if you crossed a small horn and a little flute?
Tootie flutie.

Why couldn't Noah play cards on the ark?
Because an elephant was standing on the deck.

Where do cows go for entertainment?
To the moo-vies.

What game do farm animals play?
Pig Pong.

What is long, skinny, and beats a drum?
Yankee Noodle.

What is the best way to talk
to the Frankenstein monster?
By long distance.

How do elephants
speak to each other?
On 'elephones.

How do rattlesnakes talk to each other?
Poison-to-poison.

Why wasn't the clock allowed in the library?
Because it tocked too much.

What person makes a living by talking to himself?
A ventriloquist.

What animal talks a lot?
A yak.

What animal talks the most?
A yakety yak.

Are you crazy if you talk to yourself?
Not unless you answer.

What kind of fall makes you unconscious,
but doesn't hurt you?
Falling asleep.

How can you go without sleep for
seven days and not be tired?
Sleep at night.

What is the best thing to do if
you find a gorilla in your bed?
Sleep somewhere else.

Who always goes to
sleep with shoes on?
A horse.

What question can you never answer yes to?
"Are you asleep?"

What do baby sweet potatoes sleep in?
Their yammies.

What was Dr. Jekyll's favorite game?
Hyde and Seek.

What is a zebra after it is six months old?
Seven months old.

What is black and white, black and white, black
and white and green?
Three skunks eating a pickle.

What do dogs drink at parties?
Pupsi-cola.

What kind of bow can't be tied?
A rainbow.

How do you say
goodbye to a
mummy?
"BC'ing you!"

INDEX